SCUM MANIFESTO

VALERIE SOLANAS

WITH A FOREWORD
BY MICHELLE TEA

SCUM Manifesto
By Valerie Solanas
Foreword by Michelle Tea

This edition 2013 AK Press (Oakland, Edinburgh, Baltimore)
ISBN: 978-1-84935-180-5
e-ISBN: 978-184935-181-2
Library of Congress Control Number: 2013945477

This edition based on the 1991 Phoenix Press publication which itself was based
on the 1983 Matriarchy Study Group (London) edition.

AK Press   AK Press UK
370 Ryan Ave #100   33 Tower Street
Chico, CA 95973   Edinburgh EH6 7BN
USA   Scotland
www.akpress.org   akuk.com
akpress@akpress.org   ak@akedin.demon.co.uk

The above addresses would be delighted to provide you with the latest AK Press
distribution catalog, which features several thousand books, pamphlets, zines, audio
and video recordings, and gear, all published or distributed by AK Press. Alternatively,
visit our websites to browse the catalog and find out the latest news from the world of
anarchist publishing:
www.akpress.org | www.akuk.com
revolutionbythebook.akpress.org
Printed in the United States
Cover and interior design by Morgan Buck | www.antumbradesign.org

CONTENTS

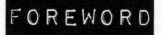
"It's hypothetical. No, hypothetical is the wrong word. It's just a literary device. There's no organization called SCUM... It's not even me... I mean, I thought of it as a state of mind. In other words, women who think a certain way are SCUM. Men who think a certain way are in the men's auxiliary of SCUM."

I was thinking a certain way when I first came across the SCUM Manifesto. I had retreated into the desert of Tucson, Arizona, in the midst of what I now refer to as my Radical Lesbian Feminist Nervous Breakdown. I make light of it, but it was a dark and dangerous moment in my life. I had just learned that my stepfather had been spying on my sister and me through holes he'd stealthily carved in the walls of our home—the bathroom walls, the bedroom walls. Throughout my teenage years I'd lived with the suspicion that this was happening, a state of mind that had me tipping on a chasm of anxiety and denial I feared might end with me going totally insane. The thing was, my stepfather was *cool*. The dad he replaced had *not* been cool, he'd been a moody alcoholic who'd fight with my mom 'til she cried. When he came home from work adulterously late and fucked-up on booze or pills, we didn't know what we'd be getting. This new dad was a *cheerful* alcoholic. He'd played drums in bands and had a pierced ear and a homemade tattoo on his finger. He was always nice to my mom, and to the rest of us. He took delight in cooking extravagant family dinners—3-alarm chili washed down with pint glasses of lime rickeys, gutted limes scattered across the kitchen table filling the house with the sharply optimistic smell of summer. How could he be spying on us?

For years I lived with the understanding that there was something wrong with me. Something dark and perverse. To see such a nice man, a man who finally loved me and my mom the way a father-person should, a man who went to the courts to adopt me, who bar-brawled with my birth-father at the local Moose Club over his love for us, his family—to know all this and then think that he's *watching* me? Sexually, I guess? What a creep. What a creep I was.

What a fishbowl my teenage bedroom was. I loved to be inside it, reading books and magazines, listening to records, sneaking cigarettes out the window. Painting band names on the linoleum with nail polish, playing with make-up, lip-synching in the mirror. I'd be wrapping my blackened mouth around the voice of Siouxsie Sioux and would suddenly freeze: *What if he was watching me right now?* My room suddenly turned eerie, spooky. I was a girl in a horror movie. There was a terrible stillness, I felt like I'd been caught. To break the spell I'd do something bizarre, or lewd—grab my crotch, squeeze my breasts, squish my face into the mirror, my tongue lolling out. I'd look like a madwoman. I wouldn't have done *that*, touched myself *there*, if I *really* thought my stepfather was watching. So I didn't *really* believe it, and by extension it wasn't happening.

Later, before sleep, I'd burrow under my neon-striped comforter to touch myself. I tried to make my face look really, really still in case he was watching. I didn't want him to know what I was doing. I tried to put my face under the covers, but felt smothered. I popped my face back out into the cool air.

He couldn't be watching. He couldn't be watching because if he was then I couldn't masturbate and I *really* wanted to masturbate. What a creep. What a creep I was.

This was a long-term, low-grade crazy, a steady hum I could live with. When I found it all to be true—that there were holes in the bathroom door that fit perfectly with a hole in the jamb, creating a tunnel that aimed your eye right at the toilet, where I would sit and pee, or poop, or smoke a stolen cigarette, or masturbate. That there were holes carved into my bedroom wall, holes a person could access by walking into the back hallway, nudging over a stray piece of paneling, pulling the electrical tape (dry and curled from being pulled so many times), and look through the hole in that wall right into the hole in my own. When I looked through that hole myself and saw it all—my bed, my posters on the wall, my clothes strewn onto the linoleum, the mirror I kneeled before, lip-synching. When it all came down I got a new, sharper crazy. I couldn't hide it like I'd hidden the schizoid feelings of being watched and being creepy. I was filled with an electric hurt, a frenzied rage. I was sick, sickened.

My mother rushed to his side, to protect him. It shouldn't have been a surprise, we had spent the past three or four years fighting weekly if not daily, about the way I looked, my white face makeup and dyed-black hair, my torn clothes. People would beat me up for looking the way I did, men and boys. I got in fist-fights or they just threw things at me from car windows, they just spit at me in the street, they just called me a freak and a slut as they sped by in their cars. That was how it went outside. Inside, it was a war with my mother, who thought I'd brought it on myself. I didn't have to look that way. And then I went queer, and that was a problem. And then the insanity I'd been staving off, *I think my dad is watching me*, erupted into reality and I sort of lost my mind.

Having to leave my house, I moved in with my girl-friend, a prostitute. Needing more than the minimum wage I was making at a Greek deli, I became one too. Notice I didn't say I "got work as a prostitute," I "found a job as a prostitute," or "was hired to do prostitution." Prostitute is not a job, it's something a woman *becomes*. My girlfriend and I would keep the phone numbers of the men we saw and crank call them after. We'd tell their wives. Make fun of what they'd wanted, make sure they understood we had not enjoyed it. Ask them to please stop call-ing prostitutes. I stole things from their homes, lit-tle things: a candle, a photograph, a toothbrush. I wanted them to feel unsafe, to become vulnerable.

I felt so unsafe—every call I went on I gathered in my mind my exit plan, what I would do if something went wrong. Would I know if a man planned to kill me? I feared my intuition was destroyed from all those years of doubting what I'd known and turning it back on myself. I scanned penises for anything that looked unhealthy, trying to keep myself safe in that way, too. None of these men would ever know anything about a life like this, a girl's life.

It was clear to me now that men could do anything they wanted. A man could move into a family and secretly get off on the daughters for years and when the truth came out, nothing really happened. He would have to deal with the shame of being caught, but he kept the house, and the daughters had to flee. He kept the wife the daughters would never again be able to trust as a mother. He came into the family like an invasive parasite, killed it, and inhabited its dead body.

I ran away to Tucson. No reason, it was just where my girlfriend wanted to go and she was all I had now. She was my housing and she shared my rage. In Tucson I worked as a prostitute and read books, feminist books. I read *The Courage to Heal*, the sexual-abuse survivor's bible. I read Mary Daly, and learned about the murdered witches, about widowed Indian women forced to fling themselves on the funereal pyre. I was learning about the global history of male violence against women and how all social systems accommodated it, from the government to my family. I started seeing so much it hurt. I started thinking that if I pushed my brain a little harder I could see into a person's mind. It scared me too much to do it but I knew that I could.

I read Andrea Dworkin's *Mercy* and the concept of killing men as a feminist action was introduced to me. A lighter read, *Lesbian Land* enchanted me with the reality that I could live in a world without men, that other women before me had begun to create these places, and that I could perhaps run to them. I visited one outside Tucson. The woman who gave us a tour was straight and brought her male lover in at night, which was okay with everyone. She slept on a mattress rigged up on a pallet and concrete blocks, right there in the middle of the desert. I saw a naked woman giving another naked woman a massage on a table set up in the shade of a mesquite tree. I met the land's owner, a sixty-something-year-old woman high up in some scaffolding, building herself an octagonal house.

I thought I would move to that land someday. Meanwhile I lived in a rented abode downtown, close enough to the University to stage "Tit-Ins" on the lawn there, inciting women to take off their shirts to protest the laws that made women keep their shirts on, sexualizing their breasts, allowing them to have the freedom to be topless only in places like strip clubs, where men could profit and get off on them. My house was close enough to downtown that I could walk to the liquor store for mescal, pausing to rip the busty St. Paulie Girl posters off the wall and dump the Slushie I bought at 7-11 on the way over the porn rack. Before I left home, I'd stopped by my mom's house and stuck Queer Nation stickers all over my step-dad's porn mags. Especially over the women who looked like me with their punky hair and ripped fishnets.

My house was close enough to frat row, that line of adobes housing frat boys, that I'd been hollered at by them passing by and learned not to turn down that street. I thought about blowing one up. I was very serious. I thought it would be fairly easy and we could probably get away with it, and if we didn't I was actually prepared to go to prison for my part in this war. Because that's what it was: a war. Men got to do anything to women and women got to walk around scared and traumatized and angry. Men got to do anything, period. Men got to do everything. Something had to take them down. The only reason I didn't blow up the frat house was that my girlfriend refused to do it with me. I didn't want to do it alone.

That would mean I was crazy. If I did it with others, I was part of a movement. Sisterhood is Powerful. I truly could have done this, could be sitting in jail right now. With an act of violence that one moment in my life—traumatized and desperate, unable to cope with what I'd experienced—could have become the rest of my life.

There's no way for me to talk about Valerie Solanas without talking about this, the trauma I experienced as a female sensitive to misogyny in this world. Valerie suffered sexual abuse from her birth father, then didn't get along with her step-father, was sent to live with a grandfather, and then her grandfather beat her up. She ran away at 15 and was impregnated by a married man—I've no understanding the nature of that relationship, but it's safe to presume it was at least statutory rape. Valerie's kid was taken away and she lived on the streets from then on.

"The effect of fathers, in sum, has been to corrode the world with maleness. The male has a negative Midas touch—everything he touches turns to shit," Valerie writes in the Manifesto. From where I sat, on my porch in Tucson, Arizona, drinking a glass of mescal and paging through, she got everything right on.

From the start, I understood the Manifesto to be totally for real and totally not. It was an ideal, a utopic vision too out-there to ever be realized, and its dense dark humor struck me as exactly correct. It was outlandish. I'd done die-ins with ACT-UP and Kiss-Ins with Queer Nation; I'd waved coat hangers at Christians trying to block clinic doors and I had a deep appreciation for the way humor was used as a device to hit the truth like a piñata, again and again, throughout the tome. To see the SCUM Manifesto's humor, to let it crack you up page after page, is not to read it as a joke. It's not. Valerie's use of humor is not unlike any novelist's use of fiction to hit at the truth. The truth of the world as seen through Valerie's eyes is patently absurd, a cosmic joke. The hilarity in the Manifesto strikes me as fighting fire with fire. Humor such as this is a muscle, a weapon. It was the truth, and the truth is so absurd it's painful.

Valerie did her work in the '60s, when it was legal for men to rape their wives, when girls who bled to death from back-alley abortions "deserved it." In 1969, a year after Valerie's famed shooting of the artist Andy Warhol, feminists who rose to speak at the New Left's Counter-Inaugural to the Nixon inauguration in Washington were greeted by audience cheers of "Take her off the stage and fuck her!" and

"Fuck her down a dark alley!" And these were the liberal-thinking men.

I've realized that going totally fucking insane is a completely rational outcome for an intelligent woman in this society, and I think this idea becomes only more solid the farther back in history you go. Says the writer Roxanne Dunbar-Ortiz, a supporter of Valerie during her dark days, "I look at someone like Dorothy Allison, who was a teenager when we started rabble-rousing, and how she testifies that it was woman's liberation that saved her life. Here's a person that was routinely raped by her stepfather for her entire childhood, and from the time she was about eight years old, lived in the most horrible conditions. She was the very kind of person who could have ended up like Valerie Solanas had women's liberation not been there."

I live in a large community of would-be Valeries— queer people, formerly or presently female, many of whom have survived the violence of the heterosexual families. Writers with sharp intellects and incredible talent whose stories are routinely rejected from the still male-dominated literary worlds, both mainstream and underground, independent and corporate. Author Red Jordan Arobateau, in a review of the eventual San Francisco production of Valerie's contested play, "Up Your Ass," writes, "The reason

I'd like to get on my knees to give Valerie a blowjob is because I identify with her and know she needed more joy. So much of my own life was hell, being a butch dike (now Transman) typing manuscripts in a hotel room, lonely, unpublished, not a dime to my name, not a friend in sight, and finding johns a lot easier to get then the love of a woman."

To be living so low yet so close to the largest artist of your time. To have caught his interest and been put in his films. All around you ideas are flying, becoming real. To be so near to power, to hand him your work, to know how he could help you, to hope that he would.

"Did you type this yourself? I'm so impressed. You should come type for us, Valerie." This is what Andy reportedly said as he received a copy of that play. That he never returned the work, the sole copy during a time before computers and Kinko's (forget about producing it), is history. The existence of "Up Your Ass" in Warhol's archives at his namesake museum in Pittsburgh suggests the artist did indeed have the work the whole time. Why didn't he just give it back to her? She probably wasn't worth his time.

Genderqueer Valerie, a big dyke. On top of everything, she walked around in her newsie hat, her scruffy hair, baggy men's clothes, cursing and smoking. It's irresistible to think of Valerie today, in 2013, when templates for so many gender identities exist. Would she be a butch dyke? A genderqueer inbetweener, bashing the gender binary? Would she transition, after all that, to male? She certainly wouldn't be the first trans man with some rabid man-hating in her past. Brilliantly minded, bold enough to present herself honestly (she took the *Village Voice* to task in 1977 for writing that she wasn't a lesbian: "I consider the part where you said, 'she's not a lesbian' to be serious libel," she said, during a time when writing about someone actually being a lesbian would be the grounds for a very profitable libel case. "The way it was worded gave the impression that I'm a heterosexual, you know?"), Valerie's understanding of gender was limited by her place and time. The Manifesto's fatal flaw is also the very thing it requires to exist—strict adherence to a binary gender system and its attendant biological determinism, all in spite of being routinely in the company of trans women such as Jackie Curtis, Holly Woodlawn, and Candy Darling, who lived in the same SRO Hotel as Valerie. Perhaps it is the influence of these women that inspired Valerie to allow for the survival of "faggots who, by their shimmering, flaming example, encourage other men to de-man themselves and thereby make themselves relatively inoffensive." I read "faggots," in this entry, to include queens and transgendered women, as there was scant consciousness about trans lives at the time, and "faggot" existed as a catch-all slur for anyone presenting as queer or genderqueer.

Again and again, as one reads the Manifesto, one asks herself, "What the hell is this?" It is so, so funny that it's hard for me not to condemn anyone bothered by it as painfully lacking a sense of humor. Check this out: "SCUM will conduct Turd Sessions, at which every male present will give a speech beginning with the sentence 'I am a turd, a lowly, abject turd' then proceed to list all the ways in which he is. His reward for doing so will be the opportunity to fraternize after the session for a whole, solid hour with the SCUM who will be present." Hilarious and begging for a performance-art enactment, but SCUM is also a very un-funny critique of American culture, then and now, delivered with the fearlessness of someone who has already been so thoroughly rejected by the system that she has nothing left to lose. Many of Valerie's notions are excellent and plausible, such as "SCUM will forcibly relieve bus drivers, cab drivers, and subway token sellers of their jobs and run buses and cabs and dispense free tokens to the public" (clearly the vision of a broke New Yorker). The Manifesto is as much of a call for a class war as a gender apocalypse, with "eliminate the money system" coming in behind overthrowing the government and before destroying the male sex in its opening mission statement. Indeed, the hysteria at a woman threatening to kill men within a culture where men kill women regularly has been so great as to even now distract from the class rage inherent to the book. Is that why Valerie never found a home among her feminist peers? Although she worked and wrote alongside the tremendous second wave feminist revolution of the '60s and '70s, writes Alice Echols in her history *Daring to Be Bad: Radical Feminism in America, 1967–1975*, "Radical feminists in New York Radical Women knew next to nothing about Solanas until she shot and nearly killed pop artist Andy Warhol in June 1968." Valerie had been to college, but every academic line she writes is followed by something completely potty-mouthed or shocking. It has less stylistically in common with feminist writings of the time and more in common with the absurdist manifestos of art movements, or with punk rock, which hadn't even happened yet. According to filmmaker Mary Harron, who went on to memorialize Valerie with the wonderful film *I Shot Andy Warhol*, the SCUM Manifesto is "deadpan, icily logical, elegantly comical: a strange juxtaposition, as if Oscar Wilde had decided to become a terrorist." Declares the Special Collections Library of Duke University, "Solanas is not generally considered to be a part of the Women's Liberation Movement." Who will claim her?

Thought she does employ the adjective "groovy" in reference to the ideal SCUM women, Valerie was certainly not a member of the moment's male-dominated anti-establishment proto-hippie counter-culture. "Dropping out is not the answer, fucking-up is," she wrote, calling bullshit on what looked like a culture of narcissistic male navel-gazing, but also she's really not a joiner: "SCUM will not picket, demonstrate, march or strike to achieve its end... SCUM will always operate on a criminal as opposed to a civil-disobedience basis." SCUM is a Manifesto written by a criminal—a queer when queer was illegal, a prostitute, a woman who looked like a man, living by her wits, an artist.

In the end, it may be the criminals, the prostitutes, and the artists who claim her. In the 1990s when I was prostituting and writing my own Manifesto in a café, I was approached by a queer woman who looked like a man who wanted to bum a piece of paper off me. I vaguely knew this person—her name was Fiver and she was part of a San Francisco dyke street gang called The HAGS. She was sitting at a table with a few other Hags, all butch dykes and all, for the record, hot. Valerie would not have looked out of place among them.

"We're making stencils," she explained. "About Valerie Solanas. You know, she wrote the SCUM Manifesto? We're going to tag them around the Tenderloin, she died in a hotel there." That's how I found out that Valerie had lived and died in my own city, from drug addiction and the poor health that comes with such an affliction, that comes with street prostitution, shitty housing, mental illness, and lack of community. I wanted to join The Hags in their Valerie crafting, but I was scared of them. They were a real gang and pulled crime and did harder drugs than I did then. They loved Valerie, and they lived and died like her. In a few years Fiver and another dyke would be killed by a batch of heroin tainted with flesh-eating bacteria. Another, Johanna, would see her mental illness flare up severely enough to keep her homeless until she died of cancer, struggling with her addiction right until the end. Another member of the gang got sober, transitioned to male, and saved his life.

This is who Valerie stood for, and these are the people who will not just remember her but cultivate a remembrance of her. This past April marked the 25th anniversary of her death, and a performance I had curated to explore her complicated legacy was canceled when an unexpected controversy grew large enough to give me concern about the safety of having such an event (plus sucked the fun out of it). Gay men accused me of giving voice to a person they likened to Hitler, Jim Jones, and Harvey Milk's assassin, the cop Dan White (all men who I believe would have fallen first to Valerie's sword). Trans women, understandably traumatized by the trans hatred in so much second-wave feminist rhetoric offered intense criticism on the internet. As time wore on, response to the event grew to a stressful clamor. The woman working the door feared for her safety, as did many of the performers—the ones who hadn't already canceled. Possibly Valerie, loyal to no demographic but her constructed, imaginary SCUM Woman, would have appreciated the hoopla, but I was frankly too exhausted and bummed out to carry on, and pulled the plug on the event, which was meant to benefit the St. James Infirmary, a free clinic in Valerie's old neighborhood that serves sex workers and trans people and could have, had it existed earlier, prevented Valerie's death at age 52.

Instead of hosting the event, I spent the evening of the 25th anniversary of Valerie's death at an artist's talk by the photographer Catherine Opie, a butch dyke whose early work documented the sexual and gender outlaws of San Francisco. In another time she could have been Valerie, a disadvantaged genderqueer artist panhandling at the edges of the art world. Today she's an art star, giving lectures at the Museum of Modern Art. It seemed the perfect start to a night that ended outside the Bristol Hotel in the Tenderloin, on the street where Valerie made her money. We drew a chalk circle on the sidewalk and stood around it with candles, each reading a piece from the Manifesto. All around us the drug-addled swayed, curious, then darted away, perhaps mistaking us for Christians or something. A woman exited the bar behind us and fell onto the ground, too drunk to walk. We posted Valerie's picture on the hotel door, and someone handed out tiny women's symbol earrings. We all put them on, all of us SCUM members whatever our gender, because as she said to the *Village Voice* in 1977, back in New York after her stint in jail and follow-up incarcerations in mental hospitals, SCUM is a state of mind. And to those of us who "think a certain way," the SCUM Manifesto will always be a fascinating, confusing document: a product of a place and time that remains sadly relevant; a piece of political literature, pre-riot grrrl riot grrrl, pre-punk punk, prescient and perturbing and revelatory. For all of its enduring controversy, or perhaps because of it, this work will be with us for the ages, to be wrestled with and fought over and never quite figured out. Congratulations Valerie, you made a work that sticks. May you rest in peace.

SCUM

MANIFESTO

Life in this society being, at best, an utter bore and no aspect of society being at all relevant to women, there remains to civic-minded, responsible, thrill-seeking females only to overthrow the government, eliminate the money system, institute complete automation, and destroy the male sex.

It is now technically feasible to reproduce without the aid of males (or, for that matter, females) and to produce only females. We must begin immediately to do so. Retaining the male has not even the dubious purpose of reproduction. The male is a biological accident: the Y (male) gene is an incomplete X (female) gene, that is, it has an incomplete set of chromosomes. In other words, the male is an incomplete female, a walking abortion, aborted at the gene stage. To be male is to be deficient, emotionally limited; maleness is a deficiency disease and males are emotional cripples.

The male is completely egocentric, trapped inside himself, incapable of empathizing or identifying with others, of love, friendship, affection, or tenderness. He is a completely isolated unit, incapable of rapport with anyone. His responses are entirely visceral, not cerebral; his intelligence is a mere tool in the services of his drives and needs; he is incapable of mental passion, mental interaction; he can't relate to anything other than his own physical sensations. He is a half-dead, unresponsive lump, incapable of giving or receiving pleasure or happiness; consequently, he is at best an utter bore, an inoffensive blob, since only those capable of absorption in others can be charming. He is trapped in a twilight zone halfway between humans and apes, and is far worse off than the apes because, unlike the apes, he is capable of a large array of negative feelings—hate, jealousy, contempt, disgust, guilt, shame, doubt—and moreover, he is *aware* of what he is and isn't.

Although completely physical, the male is unfit even for stud service. Even assuming mechanical proficiency, which few men have, he is, first of all, incapable of zestfully, lustfully, tearing off a piece, but instead is eaten up with guilt, shame, fear, and insecurity, feelings rooted in male nature, which the most enlightened training can only minimize; second, the physical feeling he attains is next to nothing; and third, he is not empathizing with his partner, but is obsessed with how he's doing, turning in an A performance, doing a good plumbing job. To call a man an animal is to flatter him; he's a machine, a walking dildo. It's often said that men use women. Use them for what? Surely not pleasure.

Eaten up with guilt, shame, fears, and insecurities and obtaining, if he's lucky, a barely perceptible physical feeling, the male is, nonetheless, obsessed with screwing; he'll swim through a river of snot, wade nostril-deep through a mile of vomit, if he thinks there'll be a friendly pussy awaiting him. He'll screw a woman he despises, any snaggle-toothed hag, and furthermore, pay for the opportunity. Why? Relieving physical tension isn't the answer, as masturbation suffices for that. It's not ego satisfaction; that doesn't explain screwing corpses and babies.

Completely egocentric, unable to relate, empathize, or identify, and filled with a vast, pervasive, diffuse sexuality, the male is pyschically passive. He hates his passivity, so he projects it onto women, defines the make as active, then sets out to prove that he is ("prove that he is a Man"). His main means of attempting to prove it is screwing (Big Man with a Big Dick tearing off a Big Piece). Since he's attempting to prove an error, he must "prove" it again and again. Screwing, then, is a desperate, compulsive, attempt to prove he's not passive, not a woman; but he is passive and does want to be a woman.

Being an incomplete female, the male spends his life attempting to complete himself, to become female. He attempts to do this by constantly seeking out, fraternizing with, and trying to live through and fuse with the female, and by claiming as his own all female characteristics—emotional strength and independence, forcefulness, dynamism, decisiveness, coolness, objectivity, assertiveness, courage, integrity, vitality, intensity, depth of character, grooviness, etc—and projecting onto women all male traits—vanity, frivolity, triviality, weakness, etc. It should be said, though, that the male has one glaring area of superiority over the female—public relations. (He has done a brilliant job of convincing millions of women that men are women and women are men). The male claim that females find fulfillment through motherhood and sexuality reflects what males think they'd find fulfilling if they were female.

Women, in other words, don't have penis envy; men have pussy envy. When the male accepts his passivity, defines himself as a woman (males as well as females think men are women and women are men), and becomes a transvestite he loses his desire to screw (or to do anything else, for that matter; he fulfills himself as a drag queen) and gets his cock chopped off. He then achieves a continuous diffuse sexual feeling from "being a woman." Screwing is, for a man, a defense against his desire to be female. Sex is itself a sublimation.

The male, because of his obsession to compensate for not being female combined with his inability to relate and to feel compassion, has made of the world a shitpile. He is responsible for:

WAR

The male's normal method of compensation for not being female, namely, getting his Big Gun off, is grossly inadequate, as he can get it off only a very limited number of times; so he gets it off on a really massive scale, and proves to the entire world that he's a "Man." Since he has no compassion or ability to empathize or identify, proving his manhood is worth an endless amount of mutilation and suffering and an endless number of lives, including his own—his own life being worthless, he would rather go out in a blaze of glory than to plod grimly on for fifty more years.

NICENESS, POLITENESS, AND "DIGNITY"

Every man, deep down, knows he's a worthless piece of shit. Overwhelmed by a sense of animalism and deeply ashamed of it; wanting, not to express himself, but to hide from others his total physicality, total egocentricity, the hate and contempt he feels for other men, and to hide from himself the hate and contempt he suspects other men feel for him; having a crudely constructed nervous system that is easily upset by the least display of emotion or feeling, the male tries to enforce a "social" code that ensures perfect blandness, unsullied by the slightest trace or feeling or upsetting opinion. He uses terms like "copulate," "sexual congress," "have relations with" (to men "*sexual* relations" is a redundancy), overlaid with stilted manners; the suit on the chimp.

MONEY, MARRIAGE, AND PROSTITUTION: WORK AND PREVENTION OF AN AUTOMATED SOCIETY

There is no human reason for money or for anyone to work more than two or three hours a week at the very most. All non-creative jobs (practically all jobs now being done) could have been automated long ago, and in a moneyless society everyone can have as much of the best of everything as she wants. But there are non-human, male reasons for maintaining the money-work system:

1. **Pussy.** Despising his highly inadequate self, overcome with intense anxiety and a deep, profound loneliness when by his empty self, desperate to attach himself to any female in dim hopes of completing himself, in the mystical belief that by touching gold he'll turn to gold, the male craves the continuous companionship of women. The company of the lowest female is preferable to his own or that of other men, who serve only to remind him of his repulsiveness. But females, unless very young or very sick, must be coerced or bribed into male company.

2. **Supply the non-relating male with the delusion of usefulness,** and enable him to try to justify his existence by digging holes and then filling them up. Leisure time horrifies the male, who will have nothing to do but contemplate his grotesque self. Unable to relate or to love, the male must work. Females crave absorbing, emotionally satisfying, meaningful activity, but lacking the opportunity or ability for this, they prefer to idle and waste away their time in ways of their own choosing—sleeping, shopping, bowling, shooting pool, playing cards and other games, breeding, reading, walking around, daydreaming, eating, playing with themselves, popping pills, going to the movies, getting analyzed, traveling, raising dogs and cats, lolling about on the beach, swimming, watching TV, listening to

music, decorating their houses, gardening, sewing, nightclubbing, dancing, visiting, "improving their minds" (taking courses), and absorbing "culture" (lectures, plays, concerts, "arty" movies). Therefore, many females would, even assuming complete economic equality between the sexes, prefer living with males or peddling their asses on the street, thus having most of their time for themselves, to spending many hours of their days doing boring, stultifying, non-creative work for someone else, functioning as less than animals, as machines, or, at best—if able to get a "good" job—co-managing the shitpile. What will liberate women, therefore, from male control is the total elimination of the money-work system, not the attainment of economic equality with men within it.

3. **Power and control.** Unmasterful in his personal relations with women, the male attains to general masterfulness by the manipulation of money and of everything and everybody controlled by money, in other words, of everything and everybody.

4. **Love substitute.** Unable to give love or affection, the male gives money. It makes him feel motherly. The mother gives milk; he gives bread. He is the Breadwinner.

5. **Provide the male with a goal.** Incapable of enjoying the moment, the male needs something to look for-

ward to, and money provides him with an eternal, never-ending goal: Just think of what you could do with 80 trillion dollars—invest it! And in three years time you'd have 300 trillion dollars!!!

6. Provide the basis for the male's major opportunity to control and manipulate—*fatherhood.*

FATHERHOOD AND MENTAL ILLNESS (FEAR, COWARDICE, TIMIDITY, HUMILITY, INSECURITY, PASSIVITY)

Mother wants what's best for her kids; Daddy only wants what's best for Daddy, that is peace and quiet, pandering to his delusion of dignity ("respect"), a good reflection on himself (status) and the opportunity to control and manipulate, or, if he's an "enlightened" father, to "give guidance." His daughter, in addition, he wants sexually—he gives her *hand* in marriage; the other part is for him. Daddy, unlike Mother, can never give in to his kids, as he must, at all costs, preserve his delusion of decisiveness, forcefulness, always-rightness, and strength. Never getting one's way leads to lack of self-confidence in one's ability to cope with the world and to a passive acceptance of the status quo. Mother loves her kids, although she sometimes gets angry, but anger blows over quickly and even while it exists, doesn't preclude love and basic acceptance. Emotionally diseased Daddy doesn't love his kids; he approves of them—if they're "good," that is, if they're nice, "respectful," obedient, subservient to his will, quiet and not given to unseemly displays of temper that would be most upsetting to Daddy's easily disturbed male nervous system—in other words, if they're passive vegetables. If they're not "good," he doesn't get angry—not if he's a modern, "civilized" father (the old-fashioned ranting, raving brute is preferable, as he is so ridiculous he can be easily despised)—but rather express disapproval, a state that, unlike anger, endures and precludes a basic acceptance, leaving the kid with the feeling of worthlessness and a life-long obsession with being approved of; the result is fear of independent thought, as this leads to unconventional, disapproved of opinions and ways of life.

For the kid to want Daddy's approval it must respect Daddy, and being garbage, Daddy can make sure that he is respected only by remaining aloof, by distantness, by acting on the precept of "familiarity breeds contempt," which is, of course, true, if one is contemptible. By being distant and aloof, he is able to remain unknown, mysterious, and thereby, to inspire fear ("respect").

Disapproval of emotional "scenes" leads to fear of strong emotion, fear of one's own anger and hatred, and to a fear of facing reality, as facing it leads at first to anger and hatred combined with a lack of self-confidence in one's ability to cope with and change the word, or even to affect in the slightest way one's own destiny, leads to a mindless belief that the world and most people in it are nice and the most banal, trivial amusements are great fun and deeply pleasurable.

The effect of fatherhood on males, specifically, is to make them "Men," that is, highly defensive of all impulses to passivity, faggotry, and of desires to be female. Every boy wants to imitate his mother, be her, fuse with her, but Daddy forbids this; *he* is the mother; *he* gets to fuse with her. So he tells the boy, sometimes directly, sometimes indirectly, to not be a sissy, to act like a "Man." The boy, scared shitless of and "respecting" his father, complies, and becomes just like Daddy, that model of "Man"-hood, the all-American ideal—the well-behaved heterosexual dullard.

The effect of fatherhood on females is to make them male—dependent, passive, domestic, animalistic, insecure, approval and security seekers, cowardly, humble, "respectful" of authorities and men, closed, not fully responsive, half-dead, trivial, dull, conventional, flattened-out, and thoroughly contemptible. Daddy's Girl, always tense and fearful, uncool, unanalytical, lacking objectivity, appraises Daddy, and thereafter, other men, against a background of fear ("respect") and is not only unable to see the empty shell behind the facade, but accepts the male definition of himself as superior, as a female, and of herself, as inferior, as a male, which, thanks to Daddy, she really is.

It is the increase of fatherhood, resulting from the increased and more widespread affluence that fatherhood needs in order to thrive, that has caused the general increase of mindlessness and the decline of women in the United States since the 1920s. The close association of affluence with fatherhood has led, for the most part, to only the wrong girls, namely, the "privileged" middle-class girls, getting "educated."

The effect of fathers, in sum, has been to corrode the world with maleness. The male has a negative Midas Touch—everything he touches turns to shit.

SUPPRESSION OF INDIVIDUALITY, ANIMALISM (DOMESTICITY AND MOTHERHOOD), AND FUNCTIONALISM

The male is just a bunch of conditioned reflexes, incapable of a mentally-free response; he is tied to his earliest conditioning, determined completely by his past experiences. His earliest experiences are with his mother, and he is throughout his life tied to her. It never becomes completely clear to the male that he is not part of his mother, that he is he and she is she.

His greatest need is to be guided, sheltered, protected, and admired by Mama (men expect women to adore what men shrink from in horror—themselves) and, being completely physical, he yearns to spend his time (that's not spent "out in the world" grimly defending against his passivity) wallowing in basic animal activities—eating, sleeping, shitting, relaxing, and being soothed by Mama. Passive, rattle-headed Daddy's Girl, ever eager for approval, for a pat on the head, for the "respect" of any passing piece of garbage, is easily reduced to Mama, mindless ministrator to physical needs, soother of the weary, apey brow, booster of the puny ego, appreciator of the contemptible, a hot water bottle with tits.

The reduction to animals of the women of the most backward segment of society—the "privileged, educated" middle-class, the backwash of humanity—where Daddy reigns supreme, has been so thorough that they try to groove on labor pains and lie around in the most advanced nation in the world in the middle of the twentieth century with babies chomping away on their tits. It's not for the kids sake, though, that the "experts" tell women that Mama should stay home and grovel in animalism, but for Daddy's; the tits for Daddy to hang onto; the labor pains for Daddy to vicariously groove on (half dead, he needs awfully strong stimuli to make him respond).

Reducing the female to an animal, to Mama, to a male, is necessary for psychological as well as practical reasons: the male is a mere member of the species, interchangeable with every other male. He has no deep-seated individuality, which stems from what intrigues you, what outside yourself absorbs you, what you're in relation to. Completely self-absorbed, capable of being in relation only to their bodies and physical sensations, males differ from each other only to the degree and in the ways they attempt to defend against their passivity and against their desire to be female.

The female's individuality, which he is acutely aware of, but which he doesn't comprehend and isn't capable of relating to or grasping emotionally, frightens and upsets him and fills him with envy. So he denies it in her and proceeds to define everyone in terms of his or her function or use, assigning to himself, of course, the most important functions—doctor, president, scientist—therefore providing himself with an identity, if not individuality, and tries to convince himself and women (he's succeeded best at convincing women) that the female function is to bear and raise children and to relax, comfort, and boost the ego of the male; that her function is such as to make her interchangeable with every other female. In actual fact, the female function is to relate, groove, love, and be herself, irreplaceable by anyone else; the male function is to produce sperm. We now have sperm banks.

In actual fact, the female function is to explore, discover, invent, solve problems, crack jokes, make music—all with love. In other words, create a magic world.

PREVENTION OF PRIVACY

Although the male, being ashamed of what he is and almost of everything he does, insists on privacy and secrecy in all aspects of his life, he has no real *regard* for privacy. Being empty, not being a complete, separate being, having no self to groove on and needing to be constantly in female company, he sees nothing at all wrong in intruding himself on any woman's thoughts, even a total stranger's, anywhere at any time, but rather feels indignant and insulted when put down for doing so, as well as confused—he can't, for the life of him, understand why anyone would prefer so much as one minute of solitude to the company of any creep around. Wanting to become a woman, he strives to be constantly around females, which is the closest he can get to becoming one, so he created a "society" based upon the family—a male-female couple and their kids (the excuse for the family's existence), who live virtually on top of one another, unscrupulously violating the females' rights, privacy, and sanity.

ISOLATION, SUBURBS, AND PREVENTION OF COMMUNITY

Our society is not a community, but merely a collection of isolated family units. Desperately insecure, fearing his woman will leave him if she is exposed to other men or to anything remotely resembling life, the male seeks to isolate her from other men and from what little civilization there is, so he moves her out to the suburbs, a collection of self-absorbed couples and their kids. Isolation enables him to try to maintain his pretense of being an individual by becoming a "rugged individualist," a loner, equating non-cooperation and solitariness with individuality.

There is yet another reason for the male to isolate himself: every man is an island. Trapped inside himself, emotionally isolated, unable to relate, the male has a horror of civilization, people, cities, situations requiring an ability to understand and relate to people. So like a scared rabbit, he scurries off, dragging Daddy's little asshole with him to the wilderness, suburbs, or, in the case of the hippy—he's way out, Man!—all the way out to the cow pasture where he can fuck and breed undisturbed and mess around with his beads and flute.

The "hippy," whose desire to be a "Man," a "rugged individualist," isn't quite as strong as the average man's, and who, in addition, is excited by the thought of having lots of women accessible to him, rebels against the harshness of a Breadwinner's life and the monotony of one woman. In the name of sharing and cooperation, he forms a commune or tribe, which, for all its togetherness and partly because of it (the commune, being an extended family, is an extended violation of the female's rights, privacy, and sanity) is no more a community than normal "society."

A true community consists of individuals—not mere species members, not couples—respecting each others individuality and privacy, at the same time interacting with each other mentally and emotionally—free spirits in free relation to each other—and cooperating with each other to achieve common ends. Traditionalists say the basic unit of "society" is the family; "hippies" say the tribe; no one says the individual.

The "hippy" babbles on about individuality, but has no more conception of it than any other man. He desires to get back to Nature, back to the wilderness, back to the home of furry animals that he's one of, away from the city, where there is at least a trace, a bare beginning of civilization, to live at the species level, his time taken up with simple, non-intellectual activities—farming, fucking, bead stringing. The most important activity of the commune, the one upon which it is based, is gang-banging. The "hippy" is enticed to the commune mainly by the prospect of all the free pussy—the main commodity to be shared, to be had just for the asking, but, blinded by greed, he fails to anticipate all the other men he has to share with, or the jealousies and possessiveness for the pussies themselves.

Men cannot co-operate to achieve a common end, because each man's end is all the pussy for himself. The commune, therefore, is doomed to failure; each "hippy" will, in panic, grab the first simpleton who digs him and whisk her off to the suburbs as fast as he can. The male cannot progress socially, but merely swings back and forth from isolation to gang-banging.

CONFORMITY

Although he wants to be an individual, the male is scared of anything in himself that is the slightest bit different from other men, it causes him to suspect that he's not really a "Man," that he's passive and totally sexual, a highly upsetting suspicion. If other men are A and he's not, he must not be a man; he must be a fag. So he tries to affirm his "Manhood" by being like all the other men. Differentness in other men, as well as in himself, threatens him; it means *they're* fags whom he must at all costs avoid, so he tries to make sure that all other men conform.

The male dares to be different to the degree that he accepts his passivity and his desire to be female, his fagginess. The farthest out male is the drag queen, but he, although different from most men, is exactly like all the other drag queens; like the functionalist, he has an identity—he is female. He tries to define all his troubles away—but still no individuality. Not completely convinced that he's a woman, highly insecure about being sufficiently female, he conforms compulsively to the man-made feminine stereotype, ending up as nothing but a bundle of stilted mannerisms.

To be sure he's a "Man," the male must see to it that the female be clearly a "Woman," the opposite of a "Man," that is, the female must act like a faggot. And Daddy's Girl, all of whose female instincts were wrenched out of her when little, easily and obligingly adapts herself to the role.

AUTHORITY AND GOVERNMENT

Having no sense of right and wrong, no conscience, which can only stem from having an ability to empathize with others... having no faith in his non-existent self, being unnecessarily competitive, and by nature, unable to co-operate, the male feels a need for external guidance and control. So he created authorities—priests, experts, bosses, leaders, etc.—and government. Wanting the female (Mama) to guide him, but unable to accept this fact (he is, after all, a MAN), wanting to play Woman, to usurp her function as Guider and Protector, he sees to it that all authorities are male.

There's no reason why a society consisting of rational beings capable of empathizing with each other, complete and having no natural reason to compete, should have a government, laws, or leaders.

PHILOSOPHY, RELIGION, AND MORALITY BASED ON SEX

The male's inability to relate to anybody or anything makes his life pointless and meaningless (the ultimate male insight is that life is absurd), so he invented philosophy and religion. Being empty, he looks outward, not only for guidance and control, but for salvation and for the meaning of life.

Happiness being for him impossible on this earth, he invented Heaven.

For a man, having no ability to empathize with others and being totally sexual, "wrong" is sexual "license" and engaging in "deviant" ("unmanly") sexual practices, that is, not defending against his passivity and total sexuality which, if indulged, would destroy "civilization," since "civilization" is based entirely upon the male need to defend himself against these characteristics. For a woman (according to men), "wrong" is any behavior that would entice men into sexual "license"—that is, not placing male needs above her own and not being a faggot.

Religion not only provides men with a goal (Heaven) and helps keep women tied to men, but offers rituals through which he can try to expiate the guilt and shame he feels at not defending himself enough against his sexual impulses; in essence, that guilt and shame he feels at being a male.

Most men, utterly cowardly, project their inherent weaknesses onto women, label them female weaknesses and believe themselves to have female strengths; most philosophers, not quite so cowardly, face the fact that male lacks exist in men, but still can't face the fact that they exist in men only. So they label the male condition the Human Condition, post their nothingness problem, which horrifies them, as a philosophical dilemma, thereby giving stature to their animalism, grandiloquently label their nothingness their "Identity Problem," and proceed to prattle on pompously about the "Crisis of the Individual," the "Essence of Being," "Existence preceding Essence," "Existential Modes of Being," etc., etc.

A woman not only takes her identity and individuality for granted, but knows instinctively that the only wrong is to hurt others, and that the meaning of life is love.

PREJUDICE (RACIAL, ETHNIC, RELIGIOUS, ETC.)

The male needs scapegoats onto whom he can project his failings and inadequacies and upon whom he can vent his frustration at not being female. And the vicarious discriminations have the practical advantage of substantially increasing the pussy pool available to the men on top.

COMPETITION, PRESTIGE, STATUS, FORMAL EDUCATION, IGNORANCE, AND SOCIAL AND ECONOMIC CLASSES

Having an obsessive desire to be admired by

women, but no intrinsic worth, the male constructs a highly artificial society enabling him to appropriate the appearance of worth through money, prestige, "high" social class, degrees, professional position and knowledge and, by pushing as many other men as possible down professionally, socially, economically, and educationally.

The purpose of "higher" education is not to educate but to exclude as many as possible from the various professions.

The male, totally physical, incapable of mental rapport, although able to understand and use knowledge and ideas, is unable to relate to them, to grasp them emotionally: he does not value knowledge and ideas for their own sake (they're just means to ends) and, consequently, feels no need for mental companions, no need to cultivate the intellectual potentialities of others. On the contrary, the male has a vested interest in ignorance; it gives the few knowledgeable men a decided edge on the unknowledgeable ones, and besides, the male knows that an enlightened, aware female population will mean the end of him. The healthy, conceited female wants the company of equals whom she can respect and groove on; the male and the sick, insecure, un-self-confident male female crave the company of worms.

No genuine social revolution can be accomplished by the male, as the male on top wants the status quo, and all the male on the bottom wants is to be the male on top. The male "rebel" is a farce; this is the male's "society," made by *him* to satisfy *his* needs. He's never satisfied, because he's not capable of being satisfied. Ultimately, what the male "rebel" is rebelling against is being male. The male changes only when forced to do so by technology, when he has no choice, when "society" reaches the stage where he must change or die. We're at that stage now; if women don't get their asses in gear fast, we may very well all die.

PREVENTION OF CONVERSATION

Being completely self-centered and unable to relate to anything outside himself, the male's "conversation," when not about himself, is an impersonal droning on, removed from anything of human value. Male "intellectual conversation" is a strained compulsive attempt to impress the female.

Daddy's Girl, passive, adaptable, respectful of and in awe of the male, allows him to impose his hideously dull chatter on her. This is not too difficult for her, as the tension and anxiety, the lack of cool, the insecurity and self-doubt, the unsureness of her own feelings and sensations that Daddy instilled in her make her perceptions superficial and render her unable to see that the male's babble is babble; like the aesthete "appreciating" the blob that's labeled "Great Art," she believes she's grooving on what bores the shit out of her. Not only does she permit his babble to dominate, she adapts her own "conversation" accordingly.

Trained from an early childhood in niceness, politeness and "dignity," in pandering to the male need to disguise his animalism, she obligingly reduces her own "conversation" to small talk, a bland, insipid avoidance of any topic beyond the utterly trivial—or is "educated," to "intellectual" discussion, that is, impersonal discoursing on irrelevant distractions—the Gross National Product, the Common Market, the influence of Rimbaud on symbolist painting. So adept is she at pandering that it eventually becomes second nature and she continues to pander to men even when in the company of other females only.

Apart from pandering, her "conversation" is further limited by her insecurity about expressing deviant, original opinions and the self-absorption based on insecurity and that prevents her conversation from being charming. Niceness, politeness, "dignity," insecurity and self-absorption are hardly conducive to intensity and wit, qualities a conversation must have to be worthy of the name. Such conversation is hardly rampant, as only completely self-confident, arrogant, outgoing, proud, tough-minded females are capable of intense, bitchy, witty conversation.

PREVENTION OF FRIENDSHIP (LOVE)

Men have contempt for themselves, for all other men whom they contemplate more than casually and whom they do not think are females, (for example "sympathetic" analysts and "Great Artists") or agents of God and for all women who respect and pander to them: the insecure, approval-seeking, pandering male-females have contempt for themselves and for all women like them; the self-confident, swinging, thrill-seeking female females have contempt for men and for the pandering male females. In short, contempt is the order of the day.

Love is not dependency or sex, but friendship, and therefore, love can't exist between two males, between a male and a female, or between two females, one or both of whom is a mindless, insecure, pandering male; like conversation, love can exist only between two secure, free-wheeling, independent, groovy female females, since friendship is based upon respect, not contempt.

Even amongst groovy females deep friendships seldom occur in adulthood, as almost all of them are either tied up with men in order to survive economically, or bogged down in hacking their way through the jungle and in trying to keep their heads about the amorphous mass. Love can't flourish in a society based upon money and meaningless work: it requires complete economic as well as personal freedom, leisure time, and the opportunity to engage in intensely absorbing, emotionally satisfying activities which, when shared with those you respect, lead to deep friendship. Our "society" provides practically no opportunity to engage in such activities.

Having stripped the world of conversation, friendship, and love, the male offers us these paltry substitutes:

"GREAT ART" AND "CULTURE"

The male "artist" attempts to solve his dilemma of not being able to live, of not being female, by constructing a highly artificial world in which the male is heroized, that is, displays female traits, and the female is reduced to highly limited, insipid subordinate roles, that is, to being male.

The male "artistic" aim being, not to communicate (having nothing inside him he has nothing to say), but to disguise his animalism, he resorts to symbol-

49

ism and obscurity ("deep" stuff). The vast majority of people, particularly the "educated" ones, lacking faith in their own judgment, humble, respectful of authority ("Daddy knows best"), are easily conned into believing that obscurity, evasiveness, incomprehensibility, indirectness, ambiguity, and boredom are marks of depth and brilliance.

"Great Art" proves that men are superior to women, that men are women, being labeled "Great Art," almost all of which, as the anti-feminists are fond of reminding us, was created by men. We know that "Great Art" is great because male authorities have told us so, and we can't claim otherwise, as only those with exquisite sensitivities far superior to ours can perceive and appreciate the slop they appreciate.

Appreciating is the sole diversion of the "cultivated"; passive and incompetent, lacking imagination and wit, they must try to make do with that; unable to create their own diversions, to create a little world of their own, to affect in the smallest way their environments, they must accept what's given; unable to create or relate, they spectate. Absorbing "culture" is a desperate, frantic attempt to groove in an ungroovy world, to escape the horror of a sterile, mindless, existence. "Culture" provides a sop to the egos of the incompetent, a means of rationalizing passive spectating; they can pride themselves on their ability to appreciate the "finer" things, to see a jewel where this is only a turd (they want to be admired for admiring). Lacking faith in their ability to change anything, resigned to the status quo, they *have* to see beauty in turds because, so far as they can see, turds are all they'll ever have.

The veneration of "Art" and "Culture"—besides leading many women into boring, passive activity that distracts from more important and rewarding activities, from cultivating active abilities, and leads to the constant intrusion on our sensibilities of pompous dissertations on the deep beauty of this and that turd. This allows the "artist" to be setup as one possessing superior feelings, perceptions, insights, and judgments, thereby undermining the faith of insecure women in the value and validity of their own feelings, perceptions, insights, and judgments.

The male, having a very limited range of feelings, and consequently, very limited perceptions, insights, and judgments, needs the "artist" to guide him, to tell him what life is all about. But the male "artist," being totally sexual, unable to relate to anything beyond his own physical sensations, having nothing to express beyond the insight that for the male life is meaningless and absurd, cannot be an artist.

How can he who is not capable of life tell us what life is all about? A "male artist" is a contradiction in terms. A degenerate can only produce degenerate "art." The true artist is every self-confident, healthy female, and in a female society the only Art, the only Culture, will be conceited, kooky, funky, females grooving on each other and on everything else in the universe.

SEXUALITY

Sex is not part of a relationship: on the contrary, it is a solitary experience, non-creative, a gross waste of time. The female can easily—far more easily than she may think—condition away her sex drive, leaving her completely cool and cerebral and free to pursue truly worthy relationships and activities; but the male, who seems to dig women sexually and who seeks out constantly to arouse them, stimulates the highly sexed female to frenzies of lust, throwing her into a sex bag from which few women ever escape. The lecherous male excited the lustful female; he *has* to—when the female transcends her body, rises above animalism, the male, whose ego consists of his cock, will disappear.

Sex is the refuge of the mindless. And the more mindless the woman, the more deeply embedded in the male "culture," in short, the nicer she is, the more sexual she is. The nicest women in our "society" are raving sex maniacs. But, being just awfully, awfully nice, they don't, of course descend to fucking—that's uncouth—rather they make love, commune by means of their bodies and establish sensual rapport; the literary ones are attuned to the throb of Eros and attain a clutch upon the Universe; the religious have spiritual communion with the Divine Sensualism; the mystics merge with the Erotic Principle and blend with the Cosmos, and the acid heads contact their erotic cells.

On the other hand, those females least embedded in the male "Culture," the least nice, those crass and simple souls who reduce fucking to fucking, who are too childish for the grown-up world of sub-urbs, mortgages, mops, and baby shit, too selfish to raise kids and husbands, too uncivilized to give a shit for anyone's opinion of them, too arrogant to respect Daddy, the "Greats" or the deep wisdom of the Ancients, who trust only their own animal, gut-ter instincts, who equate Culture with chicks, whose sole diversion is prowling for emotional thrills and excitement, who are given to disgusting, nasty upsetting "scenes"; hateful, violent bitches given to slamming those who unduly irritate them in the teeth, who'd sink a shiv into a man's chest or ram an icepick up his asshole as soon as look at him, if they knew they could get away with it, in short, those who, by the standards of our "culture" are SCUM... these females are cool and relatively cerebral and skirting asexuality.

Unhampered by propriety, niceness, discretion, public opinion, "morals," the respect of assholes, always funky, dirty, low-down SCUM gets around... and around and around... they've seen the whole show—every bit of it—the fucking scene, the dyke scene—they've covered the whole waterfront, been under every dock and pier—the peter pier, the pussy pier... you've got to go through a lot of sex to get to anti-sex, and SCUM's been through it all, and they're now ready for a new show; they want to crawl out from other the dock, move, take off, sink out. But SCUM doesn't yet prevail; SCUM's still in the gutter of our "society," which, if it's not deflected from its present course and if the Bomb doesn't drop on it, will hump itself to death.

BOREDOM

Life in a "society" made by and for creatures who, when they are not grim and depressing are utter bores, can only be, when not grim and depressing, an utter bore.

Every male's deep-seated, secret, most hideous fear is of being discovered to be not a female, but a male, a subhuman animal. Although niceness, politeness, and "dignity" suffice to prevent his exposure on a personal level, in order to prevent the general exposure of the male sex as a whole and to maintain his unnatural dominant position in "society," the male must resort to:

1. **Censorship.** Responding reflexively to isolated words and phrases rather than cereberally to overall meanings, the male attempts to prevent the arousal and discovery of his animalism by censoring not only "pornography," but any work containing "dirty" words, no matter in what context they are used.

2. **Suppression of all ideas and knowledge** that might expose him or threaten his dominant position in "society." Much biological and psychological data is suppressed, because it is proof of the male's gross inferiority to the female. Also, the problem of mental illness will never be solved while the male maintains control, because first, men have a vested interest in it—only females who have very few of their marbles will allow males the slightest bit of control over anything, and second, the male cannot

admit to the role that fatherhood plays in causing mental illness.

3. **Exposés.** The male's chief delight in life—insofar as the tense, grim male can ever be said to delight in anything—is in exposing others. It doesn't much matter what they're exposed as, so long as they're exposed; it distracts attention from himself. Exposing others as enemy agents (Communists and Socialists) is one of his favorite pastimes, as it removes the source of the threat to him not only from himself, but from the country and the Western world. The bugs up his ass aren't in him, they're in Russia.

DISTRUST

Unable to empathize or feel affection or loyalty, being exclusively out for himself, the male has no sense of fair play; cowardly, needing constantly to pander to the female to win her approval, that he is helpless without, always on the edge lest his animalism, his maleness be discovered, always needing to cover up, he must lie constantly; being empty he has not honor or integrity—he doesn't know what those words mean. The male, in short, is treacherous, and the only appropriate attitude in a male "society" is cynicism and distrust.

UGLINESS

Being totally sexual, incapable of cerebral or aesthetic responses, totally materialistic and greedy, the male, besides inflicting on the world "Great Art," has decorated his unlandscaped cities with ugly buildings (both inside and out), ugly decors, billboards, highways, cars, garbage trucks, and, most notably, his own putrid self.

HATRED AND VIOLENCE

The male is eaten up with tension, with frustration at not being female, at not being capable of ever achieving satisfaction or pleasure of any kind; eaten up with hate—not rational hate that is directed at those who abuse or insult you—but irrational, indiscriminate hate... hatred, at bottom, of his own worthless self.

Gratuitous violence, besides "proving" he's a "Man," serves as an outlet for his hate and, in addition—the male being capable only of sexual responses and needing very strong stimuli to stimulate his half-dead self—provides him with a little sexual thrill.

DISEASE AND DEATH

All diseases are curable, and the aging process and death are due to disease; it is possible, therefore, never to age and to live forever. In fact the problems of aging and death could be solved within a few years, if an all-out, massive scientific assault were made upon the problem. This, however, will not occur within the male establishment because:

1. The many male scientists who shy away from biological research, terrified of the discovery that males are females, and show marked preference for virile, "manly" war and death programs.

2. The discouragement of many potential scientists from scientific careers by the rigidity, boringness, expensiveness, time-consumingness, and unfair exclusivity of our "higher" educational system.

3. Propaganda disseminated by insecure male professionals, who jealously guard their positions, so that only a highly select few can comprehend abstract scientific concepts.

4. Widespread lack of self-confidence brought about by the father system that discourages many talented girls from becoming scientists.

5. Lack of automation. There now exists a wealth

of data which, if sorted out and correlated, would reveal the cure for cancer and several other diseases and possibly the key to life itself. But the data is so massive it requires high speed computers to corre- late it all. The institution of computers will be delayed interminably under the male control system, since the male has a horror of being replaced by machines.

6. The money system's insatiable need for new products. Most of the few scientists around who aren't working on death programs are tied up doing research for corporations.

7. The male likes death—it excites him sexually and, already dead inside, he wants to die.

8. The bias of the money system for the least creative scientists. Most scientists come from at least rela- tively affluent families where Daddy reigns supreme.

Incapable of a positive state of happiness, which is the only thing that can justify one's existence, the male is, at best, relaxed, comfortable, neutral, and this condition is extremely short-lived, as bore- dom, a negative state, soon sets in; he is, therefore, doomed to an existence of suffering relieved only by occasional, fleeting stretches of restfulness, which state he can only achieve at the expense of some female. The male is, by his very nature, a leech, an emotional parasite and, therefore, not ethically entitled to live, as no one as the right to life at someone else's expense.

Just as humans have a prior right to existence over dogs by virtue of being more highly evolved and having a superior consciousness, so women have a prior right to existence over men. The elimination of any male is, therefore, a righteous and good act, an act highly beneficial to women as well as an act of mercy.

However, this moral issue will eventually be rendered academic by the fact that the male is gradually eliminating himself. In addition to engaging in the time-honored and classical wars and race riots, men are more and more either becoming fags or are obliterating themselves through drugs. The female, whether she likes it or not, will eventually take complete charge, if for no other reason than that she will have to—the male, for practical purposes, won't exist.

Accelerating this trend is the fact that more and more males are acquiring enlightened self-interest; they're realizing more and more that the female interest is in *their* interest, that they can live only through the female and that the more the female is encouraged to live, to fulfill herself, to be a female and not a male, the more nearly *he* lives;

he's coming to see that it's easier and more sat-
isfactory to live *through* her than to try to *become*
her and usurp her qualities, claim them as his own,
push the female down and claim that she's a male.
The fag, who accepts his maleness, that is, his passivity and total sexuality, his femininity, is also best
served by women being truly female, as it would
then be easier for him to be male, feminine. If men
were wise they would seek to become really female,
would do intensive biological research that would
lead to men, by means of operations on the brain
and nervous system, being able to be transformed
in psyche, as well as body, into women.

Whether to continue to use females for reproduction or to reproduce in the laboratory will also
become academic: what will happen when every
female, twelve and over, is routinely taking the
Pill and there are no longer any accidents? How
many women will deliberately get or (if an accident)
remain pregnant? No, Virginia, women don't just
adore being brood mares, despite what the mass of
robot, brainwashed women will say. When society
consists of only the fully conscious the answer will
be none. Should a certain percentage of women be
set aside by force to serve as brood mares for the
species? Obviously this will not do. The answer is
laboratory reproduction of babies.

As for the issue of whether or not to continue to reproduce males, it doesn't follow that because the male, like disease, has always existed among us that he should continue to exist. When genetic control is possible—and soon it will be—it goes without saying that we should produce only whole, complete beings, not physical defects or deficiencies, including emotional deficiencies, such as maleness. Just as the deliberate production of blind people would be highly immoral, so would be the deliberate production of emotional cripples.

Why produce even females? Why should there be future generations? What is their purpose? When aging and death are eliminated, why continue to reproduce? Why should we care what happens when we're dead? Why should we care that there is no younger generation to succeed us.

Eventually the natural course of events, of social evolution, will lead to total female control of the world and, subsequently, to the cessation of the production of males and, ultimately, to the cessation of the production of females.

But SCUM is impatient; SCUM is not consoled by the thought that future generations will thrive; SCUM wants to grab some thrilling living for itself. And, if a large majority of women were SCUM, they could acquire complete control of this country within a few weeks simply by withdrawing from the labor force, thereby paralyzing the entire nation. Additional measures, any one of which would be sufficient to completely disrupt the economy and everything else, would be for women to declare themselves off the money system, stop buying, just loot and simply refuse to obey all laws they don't care to obey. The police force, National Guard, Army, Navy, and Marines combined couldn't squelch a rebellion of over half the population, particularly when it's made up of people they are utterly helpless without.

If all women simply left men, refused to have any-thing to do with any of them—ever, all men, the gov-ernment, and the national economy would collapse completely. Even without leaving men, women who are aware of the extent of their superiority to and power over men, could acquire complete control over everything within a few weeks, could effect a total submission of males to females. In a sane soci-ety the male would trot along obediently after the female. The male is docile and easily led, easily sub-jected to the domination of any female who cares to dominate him. The male, in fact, wants desperately to be led by females, wants Mama in charge, wants to abandon himself to her care. But this is not a sane society, and most women are not even dimly aware of where they're at in relation to men.

The conflict, therefore, is not between females and males, but between SCUM—dominant, secure, self-confident, nasty, violent, selfish, independent, proud, thrill-seeking, free-wheeling, arrogant females, who consider themselves fit to rule the universe, who have free-wheeled to the limits of this "society" and are ready to wheel on to something far beyond what it has to offer—and nice, passive, accepting "cultivated," polite, dignified, subdued, dependent, scared, mindless, insecure, approval-seeking Daddy's Girls, who can't cope with the unknown, who want to hang back with the apes, who feel secure only with Big Daddy standing by, with a big strong man to lean on and with a fat, hairy face in the White House, who are too cowardly to face up to the hideous reality of what a man is, what Daddy is, who have cast their lot with the swine, who have adapted themselves to animalism, feel superficially comfortable with it and know no other way of "life," who have reduced their minds, thoughts, and sights to the male level, who, lacking sense, imagination, and wit can have value only in a male "society," who can have a place in the sun, or, rather, in the slime, only as soothers, ego boosters, relaxers, and breeders; who are dismissed as inconsequents by other females; who project their deficiencies, their male-ness, onto all females and see the female as worm.

But SCUM is too impatient to wait for the de-brain-washing of millions of assholes. Why should the swinging females continue to plod dismally along with the dull male ones? Why should the fates of the groovy and the creepy be intertwined? Why should the active and imaginative consult the passive and dull on social policy? Why should the independent be confined to the sewer along with the dependent who need Daddy to cling to?

A small handful of SCUM can take over the country within a year by systematically fucking up the sys-tem, selectively destroying property, and murder:

- SCUM will become members of the unwork force, the fuck-up force; they will get jobs of various kinds and unwork. For example, SCUM sales-girls will not charge for merchandise; SCUM tel-ephone operators will not charge for calls; SCUM office and factory workers, in addition to fucking up their work, will secretly destroy equipment.

- SCUM will unwork at a job until fired, then get a new job to unwork at.

- SCUM will forcibly relieve bus drivers, cab driv-ers, and subway token sellers of their jobs and run buses and cabs and dispense free tokens to the public.

- SCUM will destroy all useless and harmful objects—cars, store windows, "Great Art," etc.

- Eventually SCUM will take over the airwaves—radio and TV networks—by forcibly relieving of their jobs all radio and TV employees who would impede SCUM's entry into the broadcasting studios.

- SCUM will couple-bust—barge into mixed (male-female) couples, wherever they are, and bust them up.

SCUM will kill all men who are not in the Men's Auxiliary of SCUM. Men in the Men's Auxiliary are those men who are working diligently to eliminate themselves, men who, regardless of their motives, do good, men who are playing ball with SCUM. A few examples of the men in the Men's Auxiliary are: men who kill men; biological scientists who are working on constructive programs, as opposed to biological warfare; journalists, writers, editors, publishers, and producers who disseminate and promote ideas that will lead to the achievement of SCUM's goals; faggots who, by their shimmering, flaming example, encourage other men to de-man themselves and thereby make themselves relatively inoffensive; men who consistently give things away—money, things, services; men who tell it like it is (so far not one ever has), who put women straight, who reveal the truth about themselves, who give the mindless male females correct sentences to parrot, who tell them a woman's primary goal in life should be to squash the male sex (to aid men in this endeavor SCUM will conduct Turd Sessions, at which every male present will give a speech beginning with the sentence: "I am a turd, a lowly abject turd," then proceed to list all the ways in which he is. His reward for doing so will be the opportunity to fraternize after the session for a whole, solid hour with the SCUM who will be present. Nice, clean-living male women will be invited to the sessions to help clarify any doubts and misunderstandings they may have about the male sex; makers and promoters of sex books and movies, etc., who are hastening the day when all that will be shown on the screen will be Suck and Fuck (males, like the rats following the Pied Piper, will be lured by Pussy to their doom, will be overcome and submerged by and will eventually drown in the passive flesh that they are); drug pushers and advocates, who are hastening the dropping out of men.

Being in the Men's Auxiliary is a necessary but not a sufficient condition for making SCUM's escape list; it's not enough to do good; to save their worthless asses men must also avoid evil. A few examples of the most obnoxious or harmful types are: rapists, politicians and all who are in their service (campaigners, members of political parties, etc); lousy singers and musicians; Chairmen of Boards; Breadwinners; landlords; owners of greasy spoons and restaraunts that play Muzak; "Great Artists"; cheap pikers and welchers; cops; tycoons; scientists working on death and destruction programs or for private industry (practically all scientists); liars and phonies; disc jockies; men who intrude themselves in the slightest way on any strange female; real estate men; stock brokers; men who speak when they have nothing to say; men who sit idly on the street and mar the landscape with their presence; double dealers; flim-flam artists; litterbugs; plagiarisers; men who in the slightest way harm any female; all men in the advertising industry; psychiatrists and clinical psychologists; dishonest writers, journalists, editors, publishers, etc.; censors on both the public and private levels; all members of the armed forces, including draftees (LBJ and McNamara give orders, but servicemen carry them out) and particularly pilots (if the bomb drops, LBJ won't drop it; a pilot will). In the case of a man whose behavior falls into both the good and bad categories, an overall subjective evaluation of him will be made to determine if his behavior is, in the balance, good or bad.

It is most tempting to pick off the female "Great Artists," liars and phonies etc. along with the men, but that would be inexpedient, as it would not be clear to most of the public that the female killed was a male. All women have a fink streak in them, to a greater or lesser degree, but it stems from a lifetime of living among men. Eliminate men and women will shape up. Women are improvable; men are no, although their behavior is. When SCUM gets hot on their asses it'll shape up fast.

Simultaneously with the fucking-up, looting, couple-busting, destroying and killing, SCUM will recruit. SCUM, then, will consist of recruiters; the elite corps—the hard core activists (the fuck-ups, looters and destroyers) and the elite of the elite—the killers.

Dropping out is not the answer; fucking-up is. Most women are already dropped out; they were never in. Dropping out gives control to those few who don't drop out; dropping out is exactly what the establishment leaders want; it plays into the hands of the enemy; it strengthens the system instead of undermining it, since it is based entirely on the non-participation, passivity, apathy, and non-involvement of the mass of women. Dropping out, however, is an excellent policy for men, and SCUM will enthusiastically encourage it.

Looking inside yourself for salvation, contemplating your navel, is not, as the Drop Out people would have you believe, the answer. Happiness lies outside yourself, is achieved through interacting with others. Self-forgetfulness should be one's goal, not self-absorption. The male, capable of only the latter, makes a virtue of an irremediable fault and sets up self-absorption, not only as a good but as a Philosophical Good, and thus gets credit for being deep.

SCUM will not picket, demonstrate, march, or strike to attempt to achieve its ends. Such tactics are for nice, genteel ladies who scrupulously take only such action as is guaranteed to be ineffective. In addition, only decent, clean-living male women, highly trained in submerging themselves in the species, act on a mob basis. SCUM consists of individuals; SCUM is not a mob, a blob. Only as many SCUM will do a job as are needed for the job. Also SCUM, being cool and selfish, will not subject to getting itself rapped on the head with billy clubs; that's for the nice, "privileged, educated," middle-class ladies with a high regard for the touching faith in the essential goodness of Daddy and policemen. If SCUM ever marches, it will be over the President's stupid, sickening face; if SCUM ever strikes, it will be in the dark with a six-inch blade.

SCUM will always operate on a criminal as opposed to a civil disobedience basis, that is, as opposed to openly violating the law and going to jail in order to draw attention to an injustice. Such tactics acknowledge the rightness of the overall system and are used only to modify it slightly, change specific laws. SCUM is against the entire system, the very idea of law and government. SCUM is out to destroy the system, not attain certain rights within it. Also, SCUM—always selfish, always cool—will always aim to avoid detection and punishment. SCUM will always be furtive, sneaky, underhanded (although SCUM murders will always be known to be such).

Both destruction and killing will be selective and discriminate. SCUM is against half-crazed, indiscriminate riots, with no clear objective in mind, and in which many of your own kind are picked off. SCUM will never instigate, encourage, or participate in riots of any kind or other form of indiscriminate destruction. SCUM will coolly, furtively, stalk its prey and quietly move in for the kill. Destruction will never be such as to block off routes needed for the transportation of food or other essential supplies, contaminate or cut off the water supply, block streets and traffic to the extent that ambulances can't get through or impede the functioning of hospitals.

SCUM will keep on destroying, looting, fucking-up and killing until the money-work system no longer exists and automation is completely instituted or until enough women co-operate with SCUM to make violence unnecessary to achieve these goals, that is, until enough women either unwork or quit work, start looting, leave men, and refuse to obey all laws inappropriate to a truly civilized society. Many women will fall into line, but many others, who surrendered long ago to the enemy, who are so adapted to animalism, to maleness, that they like restrictions and restraints, don't know what to do with freedom, will continue to be toadies and door-mats, just as peasants in rice paddies remain peas-ants in rice paddies as one regime topples another. A few of the more volatile will whimper and sulk and throw their toys and dishrags on the floor, but SCUM will continue to steamroller over them.

A completely automated society can be accom-plished very simply and quickly once there is a pub-lic demand for it. The blueprints for it are already in existence, and its construction will take only a few weeks with millions of people working on it. Even though off the money system, everyone will be most happy to pitch in and get the automated society

SCUM MANIFESTO

built; it will mark the beginning of a fantastic new era, and there will be a celebration atmosphere accompanying the construction. The elimination of money and the complete institution of automation are basic to all other SCUM reforms; without these two the others can't take place; with them the others will take place very rapidly. The government will automatically collapse. With complete automation it will be possible for every woman to vote directly on every issue by means of an electronic voting machine in her house. Since the government is occupied almost entirely with regulating economic affairs and legislating against purely private matters, the elimination of money and with it the elimination of males who wish to legislate "morality" will mean there will be practically no issues to vote on.

After the elimination of money there will be no further need to kill men; they will be stripped of the only power they have over psychologically independent females. They will be able to impose themselves only on the doormats, who like to be imposed on. The rest of the women will be busy solving the few remaining unsolved problems before planning their agenda for eternity and Utopia—completely revamping educational programs so that millions of women can be trained within a few months for high level intellectual work that now requires years of training (this can be done very easily once our educational goal is to educate and not perpetuate an academic and intellectual elite); solving the problems of disease and old age and death and completely redesigning our cities and living quarters. Many women will for a while continue to think they dig men, but as they become accustomed to female society and as they become absorbed in their projects, they will eventually come to see the utter uselessnes and banality of the male.

The few remaining men can exist out their puny days dropped out on drugs or strutting around in drag or passively watching the high-powered female in action, fulfilling themselves as spectators, vicarious livers,* or breeding in the cow pasture with the toadies, or they can go off to the nearest friendly suicide center where they will be quietly, quickly, and painlessly gassed to death.

Prior to the institution of automation, to the replacement of males by machines, the male should be of use to the female, wait on her, cater to her slightest

---

*It will be electronically possible for him to tune into any specific female he wants to and follow in detail her every movement. The females will kindly, obligingly consent to this, as it won't hurt them in the slightest and it is a marvelously kind and humane way to treat their unfortunate, handicapped fellow beings.

whim, obey her every command, be totally subservient to her, exist in perfect obedience to her will, as opposed to the completely warped, degenerate situation we have now of men, not only not existing at all, cluttering up the world with their ignominious presence, but being pandered to and groveled before by the mass of females, millions of women piously worshiping the Golden Calf, the dog leading the master on a leash, when in fact the male, short of being a drag queen, is least miserable when his dogginess is recognized—no unrealistic emotional demands are made of him and the completely together female is calling the shots. Rational men want to be squashed, stepped on, crushed, and crunched, treated as the curs, the filth that they are, have their repulsiveness confirmed.

The sick, irrational men, those who attempt to defend themselves against their disgustingness, when they see SCUM barrelling down on them, will cling in terror to Big Mama with her Big Bouncy Boobies, but Boobies won't protect them against SCUM; Big Mama will be clinging to Big Daddy, who will be in the corner shitting in his forceful, dynamic pants. Men who are rational, however, won't kick or struggle or raise a distressing fuss, but will just sit back, relax, enjoy the show, and ride the waves to their demise.

VALERIE SOLANAS

COMPILED BY FREDDIE BAER
(WITH A GREAT DEAL OF
THANKS TO DONNY SMITH)

On April 9, 1936 in Ventor, New Jersey, Valerie Jean Solanas was born to Louis and Dorothy Bondo Solanas. Her father sexually molested her; sometime in the 1940's her parents divorced, and Valerie moved with her mother to Washington, D.C. In 1949 Valerie's mother married Red Moran. Rebellious and stubborn, Valerie disobeyed her parents and refused to stay in Catholic high school; in response her grandfather whipped her.

At the age of 15 in 1951, Valerie ended up on her own. She dated a sailor and may have gotten pregnant by him but still managed to graduate from high school in 1954. She was a good student at the

University of Maryland at College Park, supporting herself by working in the psychology department's animal laboratory. She did nearly a year of graduate work in psychology at University of Minnesota.

After college, Solanas panhandled and worked as a prostitute to support herself. She traveled around the country and ended up in Greenwich Village in 1966. There she wrote "Up Your Ass," a play "about a man-hating hustler and a panhandler. In one version, the woman kills the man. In another, a mother strangles her son."

Early in 1967 Solanas approached Andy Warhol at his studio, the Factory, about producing "Up Your Ass," as a play and gave him her copy of the script. At the time Warhol told the journalist Grechen Berg: "I thought the title was so wonderful and I'm so friendly that I invited her to come up with it, but it was so dirty that I think she must have been a lady cop.... We haven't seen her since and I'm not surprised. I guess she thought that was the perfect thing for Andy Warhol."

Also in 1967 Solanas wrote and self published the SCUM Manifesto. While selling mimeographed copies on the streets, she meant Maurice Girodias of Olympia Press (French publisher of *Lolita*, *Candy* and *Tropic of Cancer*) who gave her an advance for a novel based on the manifesto. (With this $600 cash she visited San Francisco.) During this time Ultra Violet read the Manifesto to Warhol who commented, "She's a hot water bottle with tits. You know, she's writing a script for us. She has a lot of ideas."

Later, in May 1967, after Warhol had returned from a trip to France and England, Solanas demanded her script back; Warhol informed her he had lost it. Apparently, Warhol had never any intention to produce "Up Your Ass" as either a play or a movie; the script was simply lost in the shuffle, thrown into one of the Factory's many stacks of unsolicited manuscripts and papers. Solanas began telephoning insistently, ordering Warhol to give her money for the play.

In July 1967 Warhol paid Solanas twenty-five dollars for performing in *I, a Man*, a feature-length film he was making with Paul Morrissey. Valerie appeared as herself, a tough lesbian who rejects the advances of a male stud with the line that she has instincts that "tell me to dig chicks—why should my standards be lower than yours?" Solanas also appeared in a non-speaking role in *Bikeboy*, another 1967 Warhol film. Warhol was pleased with her frank and funny performance; Solanas also was satisfied enough that she brought Girodias to the studio to see a rough cut of the film. Girodias noted that Solanas "seemed very relaxed and friendly with Warhol, whose conversation consisted of protracted silences."

In the fall of 1967 at the New York cafe Max's Kansas City, Warhol spotted Solanas sitting at a nearby table. He instigated Viva's insult of Solanas: "You dyke! You're disgusting!" Valerie answered with the story of her sexual abuse at the hands of her father. "No wonder your a lesbian," Viva callously replied.

Over the winter of 1967–68, Solanas was interviewed by Robert Mamorstein of the *Village Voice*. The article, "Scum Goddess: A Winter Memory of Valerie Solanas" was not published until June 13, 1968, after the shooting. Solanas commented on the men interested in SCUM: "[C]reeps. Masochists. Probably would love me to spit on them. I wouldn't give them the pleasure…. The men want to kiss my feet and all that crap." Her comment on women and sex: "The girls are okay. They're willing to help any way they can. Some of them are interested in nothing but sex though. Sex with me, I mean. I can't be bothered …. I'm no lesbian. I haven't got time for sex of any kind. That's a hang-up." She told Mamorstein that Warhol was a son of a bitch: "A snake couldn't eat a meal off what he paid out." Solanas also talked about her life; she had surfed as a little girl. She panhandled and even sold an article on panhandling to a magazine. "I've had some funny experiences with strange guys in cars."

According to the interview, she wrote a few sex novels and was paid $500 for one. (Could this have been the novel that was to have been based on the SCUM Manifesto?) She was interviewed on Alan Burke's TV talk show; when she refused to censor herself, he walked off the set. The interview was never aired. According to Paul Morrissey in a 1996 interview with Taylor Mead, the contract that Solanas signed with Olympia Press "this stupid piece of paper, two sentences, tiny little letter." On it Maurice Girodias said: "I will give you five hundred dollars, and you will give me your next writing, and other writings." Solanas had interpreted it to mean that Girodias would own every thing she ever wrote. She told Morrissey: "Oh no, everything I write will be his. He's done this to me, He's screwed me!" Morrissey believed Solanas couldn't write the novel based on the SCUM Manifesto she had promised to Girodias and used this idea that Girodias owned all that she wrote as an excuse. In Solanas's mind, Warhol, having appropriated "Up Your Ass," wanted Girodias to steal her work for Warhol's use and never pay her so he got Girodias to sign this contract with her.

In the spring of 1968, Solanas approached under-ground newspaper publisher (*The Realist*) Paul Krassner for money, saying "I want to shoot Maurice Girodias." He gave her $50, enough for a .32 automatic pistol.

On June 3, 1968 at 9AM Solanas went to the Chelsea Hotel where Maurice Girodias lived: she asked at the desk for him and was told that he was gone for the weekend. Still, she remained there for three hours. Around noon she went to the newly relocated Factory and waited outside for Warhol. Paul Morrissey met her in front and asked her what she was doing there. "I'm waiting for Andy to get money," she replied. To get rid of her, Morrissey told her that Warhol wasn't coming in that day. "Well that's alright. I'll wait," she said.

About 2PM she came up to the studio in the ele-vator. Once again Morrissey told her that Warhol wasn't coming and that she couldn't hang around so she left. She came up the elevator another seven times before she finally came up with Warhol at 4:15. She was dressed in a black turtleneck sweater and a raincoat, with her hair styled and wearing lip-stick and make-up; she carried a brown paper bag. Warhol even commented "Look, doesn't Varlerie look good!" Morrissey told her to get out: "We got business, and if you don't go I'm gonna beat the hell

out of you and throw you out, and I don't want..."
Then the phone rang; Morrissey answered—it was
Viva, for Warhol. Morrissey then excused himself
to go to the bathroom. As Warhol spoke on the
phone, Solanas shot him three times. Between the
first and second shot, both of which missed, Warhol
screamed, "No! No! Valarie, don't do it." Her third
shot sent a bullet through Warhol's left lung, spleen,
stomach, liver, esophagus, and right lung.

As Warhol lay bleeding, Solanas then fired twice
upon Mario Amaya, an art critic and curator who
had been waiting to meet Warhol. She hit him
above the right hip with her fifth shot; he ran from
the room to the back studio and leaned against
the door. Solanas then turned to Fred Hughes,
Warhol's manager, put her gun to his head and
fired; the gun jammed. At that point the elevator
door opened; there was no one on it. Hughes said
to Solanas, "Oh, there's the elevator. Why don't
you get on, Valerie?" She replied: "That's a good
idea," and left.

That evening at 8PM Solanas turned herself in to a
rookie traffic officer in Time Square; she said, "The
police are looking for me and want me." She then
took the .32 automatic and a .22 pistol from the
pockets of her raincoat, handing them to the cop.
As she did so, she stated that she had shot Andy

Warhol and in way of explanation offered, "He had too much control of my life."

A mob of journalists and photographers shouting questions greeted Solanas as she was brought to the 13th Precinct booking room. When asked why she did it, her response was, "I have lots of reasons. Read my manifesto and it will tell you who I am." Solanas was fingerprinted and charged with felonious assault and possession of a deadly weapon.

Later that night Valerie Solanas was brought before Manhattan Criminal Court Judge David Getzoff. She told the judge: "It's not often that I shoot somebody. I didn't do it for nothing. Warhol had me tied up, lock stock, and barrel. He was going to do something to me which would have ruined me." When the judge asked if she could afford an attorney, she replied: "No, I can't. I want to defend myself. This is going to stay in my own competent hands. I was right in what I did! I have nothing to regret!" The judge struck her comments from the court record, and Solanas was taken to the Bellevue Hospital psychiatric ward for observation.

On June 13, 1968 Valerie Solanas appeared in front of State Surpreme Court Justice Thomas Dickens; she was then represented by radical feminist lawyer Florynce Kennedy who called Solanas "one of the most important spokeswomen of the feminist movement." Kennedy asked for a writ of *habeas corpus* because Solanas was inapproriately held in a psychiatric ward, but the judge denied the motion and sent Solanas back to Bellevue. Ti-Grace Atkinson, the New York chapter president of NOW, attended Solanas's court appearance and said she was "the first outstanding champion of women's rights."

On June 28 Solanas was indicted on charges of attempted murder, assault, and illegal possession of a gun. In August, Solanas was declared incompetent and was sent to Ward Island Hospital. August 1968, Olympia Press published the SCUM Manifesto with essays by Maurice Girodias and Paul Krassner.

The night before Christmas 1968: Warhol answered the phone at the factory; it was Solanas calling. She demanded that Warhol pay $20,000 for her manuscripts that she would use for her legal defense.She wanted him to drop all criminal charges against her, put her in more of his movies and get her on the Johnny Carson Show. Solanas said if Warhol didn't do this, she "could always do it again."

June 1969: After pleading guilty, Valerie Solanas was sentenced to three years in prison for "reckless assault with intent to harm"; the year she spent in a psychi-

atric ward awaiting trial counted as time served. It
has been suggested that Warhol's refusal to testify
against Solanas contributed to the short sentence.

Solanas was released on September 1971 from the
New York State Prison for Women at Bedford Hills;
she was arrested again November 1971 for threatening letters and calls to various people, including
Andy Warhol. In 1973 Solanas was in and out of
mental institutions; she spent eight months in South
Florida State Hospital in 1975.

In the July 25, 1977 *Village Voice*, Howard Smith
interviewed Valerie Solanas. She claimed to be
working on a new book, about her life "bullshit,"
titled *Valerie Solanas*. She was supposed to have
received $100,000,000 in advance from "The
Mob", whom she describes as "the Money Men;"
she talked at length about "the Contact Man" for
this entity.

In the interview she discussed the Society for Cutting
Up Men: "It's hypothetical. No, hypothetical is the
wrong word. It's just a literary device. There's no
organization called SCUM...." Smith: "It's just you."
Solanas: "It's not even me... I mean, I thought of
it as a state of mind. In other words, women who
think a certain way are in SCUM. Men who think a
certain way are in the men's auxiliary of SCUM."

She also protested a 1968 statement of Smith's: "The part where you said, 'She's a man-hater, not a lesbian'…. I thought that was just totally unwarranted. Because I have been a lesbian… Although at the time time I wasn't sexual, I was into all kinds of other things…. The way it was worded gave the impression that I'm a heterosexual, you know…. "

The next issue of the *Village Voice* on August 1, 1977 has another piece by Howard Smith, "Valerie Solanas Replies." In it Solanas corrected misinterpretations from previous issue's interview. Included are:

1) Olympia Press's editions of the Manifesto were inaccurate, "words and even extended parts of sentences left out, rendering the passages they should have been in incoherent;" and

2) The Voice refused to publish the address of the Contact Man, which she considered one of the important reasons for the interview. She called Smith journalistically immoral and said "I go by an absolute moral standard."… Smith: "Valerie do you want to get into a discussion now about shooting people?" Solanas: "I consider that a moral act. And I consider it immoral that I missed. I should have done target practice."

Also in 1977 she mailed a rambling letter to a *Playboy* editor on the theory that he was a contact man for The Mob. Then there is no record of Solanas until November 1987 when Ultra Violet tracked her down in Northern California. When Ultra telephoned her, Solanas didn't have much to say.

April 26, 1988: broke and alone, Valerie Solanas died of emphysema and pneumonia in a welfare hotel in the Tenderloin district of San Francisco. When she died at the age of 52, she had a drug problem and continued to turn tricks to support her habit. Prostitutes who knew her from that time said that she looked elegant and slender, and she always wore a silver lamé dress when she worked the street.

In a January 14, 1991 *New York* magazine article, "Andy Warhol's Feminists Nightmare," Rowan Gaither interviewed Dorothy Moran, Solanas's mother, who denied reports of Valerie's later years: "Solanas lived peacefully in New York during the seventies and later in Phoenix and San Francisco. 'I think she had some good friends that helped her out a lot.'" Moran rejected the idea that Solanas was in and out of mental institutions during the 1970s: "She was writing. She fancied herself as a writer, and I think she did have some talent. For years, she even lived with a man…. She had a terrific sense of humor."

She was buried in Virginia, near the home of her mother.

ABOUT AK PRESS

AK Press is small, in terms of staff and resources, but we also manage to be one of the world's most productive anarchist publishing houses. We publish close to twenty books every year, and distribute thousands of other titles published by like-minded independent presses and projects from around the globe. We're entirely worker-run and democratically managed. We operate without a corporate structure—no boss, no managers, no bullshit.

The Friends of AK program is a way you can directly contribute to the continued existence of AK Press, and ensure that we're able to keep publishing books like this one! Friends pay $25 a month directly into our publishing account ($30 for Canada, $35 for international), and receive a copy of every book AK Press publishes for the duration of their membership! Friends also receive a discount on anything they order from our website or buy at a table: 50% on AK titles, and 20% on everything else. We have a Friends of AK ebook program as well: $15 a month gets you an electronic copy of every book we publish for the duration of your membership. You can even sponsor a very discounted membership for someone in prison.

Email friendsofak@akpress.org for more info, or visit the Friends of AK Press website: https://www.akpress.org/friends.html

There are always great book projects in the works—so sign up now to become a Friend of AK Press, and let the presses roll!